modern
shibori

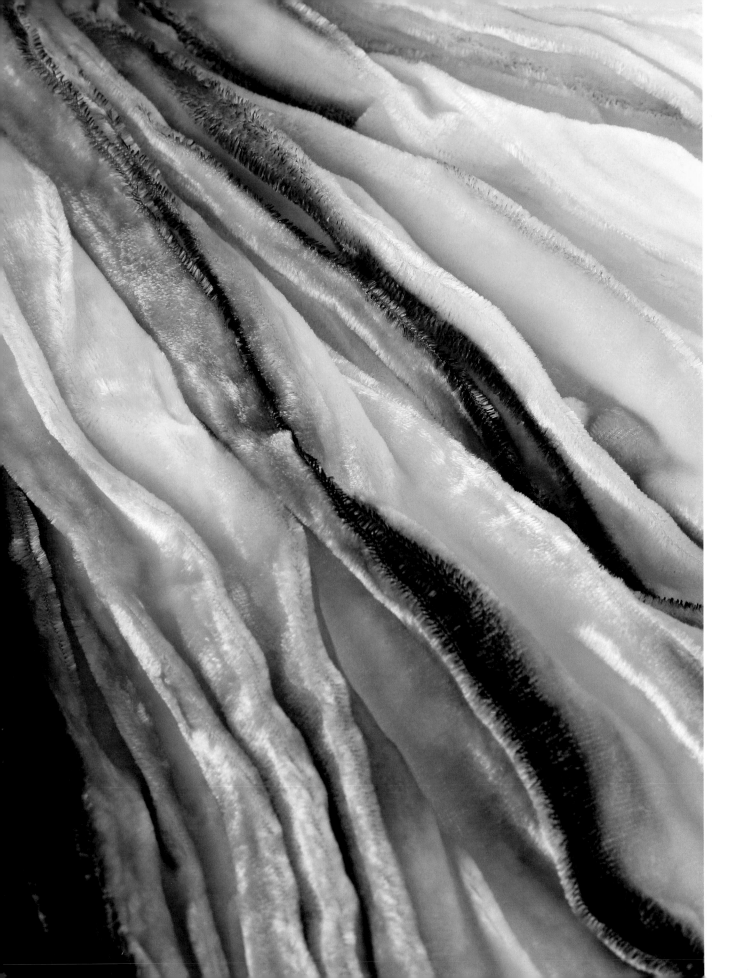

Silke Bosbach

modern shibori

A & C Black · London

CONTENTS

SHIBORI TECHNIQUES

GALLERY OF PROJECTS

Shibori – Between Tradition and Modernity

Shibori was originally an art form of the poor. In feudal Japan not everyone could afford expensive materials such as cotton or silk, and for that reason clothing was made from cheap hemp. Many people were too poor to make new clothes even when they were needed, so they patched them up and dyed them a new colour. The original art of shibori lay in making old clothes look new again.

Shibori is a Japanese expression, a generic term covering a wide range of highly specialised, esoteric procedures. The essential principle of this traditional technique is that through the binding, compressing, squeezing, folding and subsequent colouring of basic textiles, a pattern is allowed to emerge. These diverse traditional methods of control are what allow the dye colours to penetrate the material in such distinctive ways, with gorgeous patterns and delicate contours combining with three-dimensional forms. The basic materials, today just as in the past, are fabric and thread. Added to that, another key ingredient is the dexterity essential for the detailed hand- or more specifically finger-work required of this technique.

Various shibori techniques have been and still are used in other regions around the world, but under different names. Binding materials in this way is called in Japan, for example, 'kanoko shibori', in Nigeria 'adire eleso', in Indonesia 'plangi', and in India 'bandhani'. Accordingly, there are also terms for sewing, folding and rolling techniques. In English, shibori is tradionally known as 'tie-dye', but is sometimes wrongly referred to as 'tied batik', although 'batik' normally means a dyeing process employing wax resist.

In Western Europe shibori has been changed by the discovery and development of new materials and technologies. So it comes as no surprise that these techniques, with their capacity for creating form and meaning, have won over artists and designers. However, it has been the case for some time that the basic material for a piece of shibori need not be one that was part of the original tradition. Instead, nowadays non-textile materials, such as fine PVC foils and wire, are also used to make these forms. But the intention of this book is to emphasize that modern shibori is not just a technique for textile designers and artists. Anyone interested in fabrics, colours and colouring techniques can discover new things here, and try out the techniques for themselves.

Finally, a word about the projects: all the objects in this book have a title oriented towards the philosophy of the Five Elements – a sense of how to describe nature that is found in Daoism and also in Buddhism.

So enter the world of modern shibori and experiment with fabrics and colours.

Silke Bosbach

MATERIALS

The modern shibori being produced today captivates by its ability to create clear meaning through simple design. This stems from, among other things, the few basic materials needed to create a piece of shibori.

These few materials, however, should be carefully selected and precisely placed. To make a meaningful and attractive piece of shibori you really need only four basic materials and a few additional resources. The four basic materials are:

- Textile or non-textile base materials
- Strings for binding and materials for wrapping round
- Filling material
- Colour products

ON
live

TREND-COLLECTION
LINIE 231
FILZ-WOLLE

50 GRAMM

100% Schurwolle
virgin wool

∼ ca. 50 Meter

✂ 8,0

Ideal zum Filzen
in der Waschmaschine

www.online-garne.de
EIN PRODUKT DER
ONLINE
KLAUS KOCH GMBH
D-35260 STADTALLENDORF

Textile base materials

Silk

Silk is actually a traditional material, though also one that in our time is enjoying a significant revival as a modern medium for shibori practitioners.

Silk threads, produced by silk spinners and derived from a number of different natural protein substances, are woven into silk fabrics. These fabrics vary in quality, each having different characteristics of weave, smoothness and surface structure that can be exploited. Silk, besides being conventionally available by the metre in various lengths and widths, can also be obtained from shops specializing in finished, handmade shawls and scarves.

The four ideal types of silk for modern shibori are:

Chiffon: A particularly fine-threaded, delicate weave with a muted matt sheen.

Pongee silk (particularly in the thinner strengths 05 and 06): A light and smooth silk type, in modern shibori it is suitable for use with wrapping techniques.

Crêpe satin: A fabric that is very shiny on one side and duller on the other. Dyed shibori pieces in this material look especially radiant and intense.

However, it can happen that the thicker quality of the material means that the textile colour does not spread evenly and the colour results differ from one piece of fabric to the next.

Stainless-steel silk: For some time now, specialist shops have been offering a stainless-steel silk weave (79% steel and 21% silk). This combination of materials allows you to create durable 3D effects in your textile base through the simplest shibori techniques.

Etamine

The term 'etamine' stems from the French and roughly translates as 'muslin wool', though etamine is the standard term in English. The material is lightweight and is at first porous, but putting it in the washing machine turns it into a smooth, soft, felted pure wool fabric that lends itself well to use with colour products.

Etamine is available either in its raw, undyed state, or else pre-coloured. The colour range of dyed fabrics available from a dealer is wide enough to cover any colour you may wish for, so that you need not do any of your own colouring if you don't want to.

Raw etamine is washed and at first has quite a rough texture, even though it is made exclusively from the finest virgin wool. But a hot wash in the machine will transform it into something soft and cosy.

Felt

To begin with, we need to differentiate between milled felt and needle felt. Both types are available in different lengths, widths, thicknesses and colours. The main advantage of felt lies in its ability to dampen down noise, and it is also incredibly well suited to making objects to decorate interior spaces.

Milled felt (also known as wool felt) is derived from animal hair or sheep's wool. The material is produced by rubbing (with circular hand movements), pressure, heat and moisture. The wool fibres, because of their scaly structure, should become entangled with one another. The pressing and squashing together of these fibres will produce felt.

Needle felts can be made from natural fibres but also from synthetic fibres. The fibres combine with one another through being worked on mechanically with a needle.

Felt can be shrunk in the washing machine on a 30°C (86°F) setting, with great results. You can exploit this quality when making modern shibori.

Wool fleece

In recent years thin and light fleeces have been increasingly favoured in textile design over felt.

Source material for fleece fabric can be made from either natural or synthetic fibres, and these can be produced through a range of processes – chemical, thermal or mechanical.

Compared to felts, as a rule fleeces are only 3mm (⅛in) thick and thus are more lightweight. You can get them from specialist shops in many different colours, lengths and widths.

Wool fleece can be exposed, using the washing machine, to temperatures over 30°C (86°F), whereupon it will shrink. This process should be used for modern shibori.

Knitted fabric

You can also use hand-knitted fabric for contemporary shibori. This is known as knitted felt.

Making knitted felt is very easy: you put a knitted fabric in the washing machine and take out a felt object. The knitted piece will shrink in the washing machine at any temperature of 30° (86°F) or more. How much the wool shrinks depends on the kind of thread used in the fabric and also on the temperature at which you wash it.

It is important, however, that the basic wool you choose is one that can be felted. Superwash yarn, cotton threads, silk, polyester and polyamide threads, and microfibre threads are just some of the types of thread that are unsuitable for felting.

Cotton

Cotton is a natural fibre obtained from the fibre bolls, or capsules, that grow around the seeds of the cotton plant. The plant seeds form longer hairs (raw cotton lint) which are mostly spun into thin threads and used in making textiles.

TIP

Prepare various knitted test pieces and wash them at different temperatures in the washing machine, so that you get a better idea of how much the wool will shrink at a given temperature.

Cotton can absorb up to 65% of its own weight in water, though it also takes a long time to dry out. Cotton doesn't irritate the skin – indeed is very kind to it, and has a low potential for allergy reactions – and thus is highly prized by the textile industry. Cotton fibre is either creamy white or dirty grey depending on the manufacturing process.

Batiste

Batiste refers to a fine threaded woven cloth with a delicate texture. The source material is predominantly cotton, but partly also manmade fibre, linen, silk or viscose. Batiste is available as bleached or multicolour-printed.

In all probability this fabric was developed by the linen weaver Jean Baptiste, in Cambrai in north-eastern France, in the 13th century. The lamps on pages 106 and 110 are made from silk, but they can also be produced using batiste.

Gauze

Gauze, also known as mull, is a semi-transparent, light weave. The term 'gauze' comes from the French, which in turn is likely to have originated from the Arabic word 'qazz' meaning 'raw silk'. A connection to the city of Gaza, where for a long time this weave was produced, is also possible.

Non-textile base materials

The term 'mull' refers to a thin, soft, plain muslin, and comes from the Hindi word meaning 'very soft'. Gauze is also very good for making the lamps on pages 106 and 110.

Foil

The word 'foil' derives from the medieval word *folia*, meaning 'leaves'. These days thin sheet metals such as silver foil, gold leaf or aluminium are all regarded as foils. But fine leaves made of synthetic materials can also be described by the term.

Synthetic foils made from numerous source materials are available in gorgeous finishes. To achieve particular effects you can use wafer-thin decorator's polythene dust sheets, which can be worked on with a wide variety of shibori techniques.

Imitation leather

Imitation leather, or vinyl, is successfully used in clothing, furniture and shoes. You often find polyamide or polyester indicated in certain types of imitation leather. The ability of this material to hold a structure makes it suitable to use directly in creating shibori objects with minimal effort. Imitation leather usually has a textile reverse side with a synthetic coating. It melts under heat, for example from an embossing torch or by putting it in the washing machine. This characteristic can be exploited in shibori binding techniques.

Fly screen

A fly screen is usually made from a fine textile of wire mesh with a mesh size of approximately 1mm (US mesh size 18). Good fly screens are available in a synthetic-coated fibreglass mesh with a mesh width of about 1.4 x 1.2mm (US mesh size 14/16). Fibreglass mesh is extremely weatherproof, which allows for the making of modern shibori pieces that can withstand the elements if placed outdoors. Fly screen is available in numerous lengths and widths.

Strings for binding and wrapping materials

Modern shibori is served by a multitude of techniques, for use in sewing, tying or wrapping up textile or non-textile base materials with threads or other materials. However, it is important that the material used is appropriate to the method chosen, so that the full effect can be achieved.

For binding techniques used in making shibori pieces that will later be unbound, it is recommended that you use material that doesn't cost too much – for example, nylon or sisal. With other shibori techniques, any materials applied to a non-textile base material that will be a permanent feature of the piece should be durable in the long term.

Nylon string

Binding string serves to fix in specific places objects created from gathering up the textile or non-textile base materials used in modern shibori. Nylon strings, which exhibit a high tensile strength, are very well suited to this task, and are commercially available in various natural shades. They are coated with microcrystalline wax and are temperature-resistant up to 70°C (158°F). Nylon strings are mostly silicon-free and are non-corrosive to copper.

Pinja ribbon

Pinja ribbon is made from 100% cotton and is available in two different strengths – narrow and wide. It is shrink-resistant and after washing should be laid flat, or hung up, for drying. It is suitable for use as a binding or wrapping material as it is versatile, easy to work with and nice to handle. The wide Pinja ribbon is available in 16 different colours, and the narrow one in nine. In modern shibori work it can be used for wrapping but also as a filling material.

Metallic thread

Metallic threads are used when you want the binding or wrapping materials to be permanently fixed to the textile or non-textile base materials.

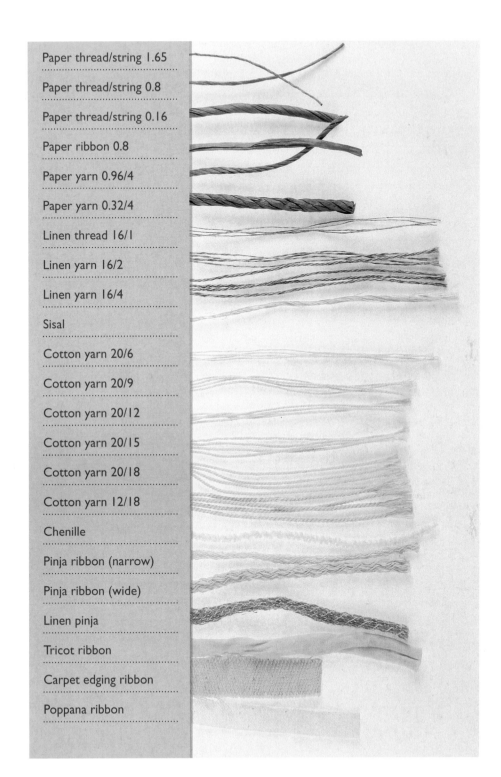

Paper thread/string 1.65
Paper thread/string 0.8
Paper thread/string 0.16
Paper ribbon 0.8
Paper yarn 0.96/4
Paper yarn 0.32/4
Linen thread 16/1
Linen yarn 16/2
Linen yarn 16/4
Sisal
Cotton yarn 20/6
Cotton yarn 20/9
Cotton yarn 20/12
Cotton yarn 20/15
Cotton yarn 20/18
Cotton yarn 12/18
Chenille
Pinja ribbon (narrow)
Pinja ribbon (wide)
Linen pinja
Tricot ribbon
Carpet edging ribbon
Poppana ribbon

Nowadays there are many different threads with various effects. For the objects in this book, Madeira lamé metallic thread was used. It consists of 65% viscose and 35% polyester with a metallic effect. The metallic thread is soft, is excellent to work with and to wear, and is available in 16 colours.

Paper thread/paper string

Paper thread, also known as paper string, is used in modern shibori in the same way as metallic thread, namely on those occasions when the binding strings are intended to be permanent features of the work – for example, in the case of the lamps on pages 106 and 110.

Industrial paper threads or strings mostly have a slippery, dust-free, slightly shiny surface, and are available in various thread strengths. In its twisted and dry state paper thread demonstrates enormous strength, though as it takes on moisture this strength is considerably reduced (until at 40% moisture content it is no longer usable). Almost unbelievable, but true!

The strengths of paper thread or string are indicated by the unit of measurement Nm (which stands for metric number). The figure denotes how many metres of thread or string there are per gram in weight. The thread or string is available from specialist shops in the form of cords, as well as wound onto spools and cones.

Paper threads or strings suitable for shibori are those with a simple twist in strengths of Nm 0.8, Nm 0.16 and Nm 1.65, all of which are good for knotting. Beyond this, the fineness of these materials lends the finished shibori piece a very plain aesthetic, even when thin paper thread or string of Nm 1.65 (interwoven with gold and silver threads) is used.

It is best to use paper threads or strings from Finland called 'Pirkanmann Kotityö', also known as 'Pirkka'. Since 1955, these have been produced in the Finnish city of Tampere and they are also dyed by the same company at their own dyeing works.

Wire

You can also use wire in shibori pieces for binding and wrapping textile and non-textile base materials. Wire usually consists of flexible metal and has a round cross section. Alternatively, specialist shops also offer wire in flat, square or specially designed profiles. Its length means that it is sold in the form of rolls or spools. Metals used in producing wire are copper, iron, brass, gold, silver, aluminium and even stainless steel.

Filling materials

In the various shibori techniques, different materials are used for filling or stuffing both the textile and non-textile base materials.

Pulses

Dried pulses such as beans, lentils or peas are the original and in the main the most reasonable materials for filling and binding in modern shibori practice. However, it is worth noting that pulses should not be left in situ in the piece when the material is being washed or dyed. Dried pulses swell naturally in water, increasing in volume, and can lead to an undesirable colour change in any textile base material.

Glass and wood pearls

In addition to pulses, you can also insert other articles, such as glass or wood pearls, as filling. These are available in numerous sizes and shapes, from spherical to cuboid.

Glass pearls can be worked as a permanent fixture into modern shibori pieces made from transparent or semi-transparent base materials.

Wood pearls are mostly cheaper than glass pearls. When working with shibori techniques involving water, undyed or varnished wood pearls or wood products should be inserted into the textile or non-textile base materials, to avoid the danger of leaving behind unsightly colour traces.

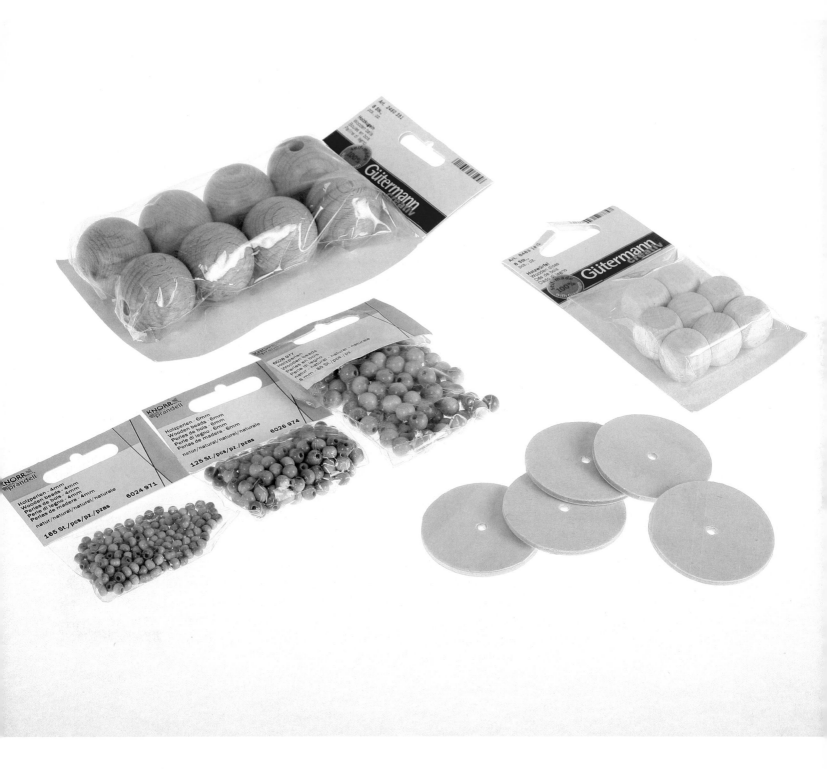

Other materials

Other **wood**, **glass** or **plastic materials** can be used for shibori techniques. These would include wooden dowels and children's wooden blocks, and even the wooden or plastic figures used in board games.

Wonderful effects can also be achieved by using **glass nuggets** or **pebbles** (which come in various shapes, sizes and colours) with shibori wrapping techniques. A recent development has been specially moulded nuggets with, for example, recognisable motifs or faces on their surfaces. They draw attention to themselves when worked into non-textile base materials and also delicate, transparent fabrics.

Sealed foil objects filled with water create a marvellous effect when wrapped around certain shibori art objects (see the Water project on page 78).

Nails are made out of metals such as steel, copper or brass, or even out of wood, and are normally forced into a workpiece or component with a hammer. In the context of shibori they can be an effect in their own right when worked into non-textile base materials, either in their untreated form or varnish-coated, or coloured with acrylic (one colour or multicoloured). When bound into non-textile materials, they give rise to wonderful contrasts. Screws can also be used in this unfamiliar way.

Colour products

Many traditional shibori techniques past and present used indigo dye. Indigo is a deep blue, or more particularly bluey-violet, colour substance derived from the Indian indigo plant, but also from German *Färbenwaid* (*Isatis tinctora*), in English known as German indigo or dye woad. Today's indigo colours are mostly chemically produced.

Modern shibori, however, is served by numerous newly developed colour products. Hobby and craft shops stock a multitude of colour products that offer a quick and uncomplicated range of possibilities for colouring textiles. These include cold-water batik textile dye, hot-water batik textile dye, silk-painting colours and iDye products. When buying colour products, don't pay too much attention to the product title, but read instead the more detailed information given on the packaging to see whether or not it is suitable for use with your chosen material. It is not always possible to dye natural and synthetic material with the same dye.

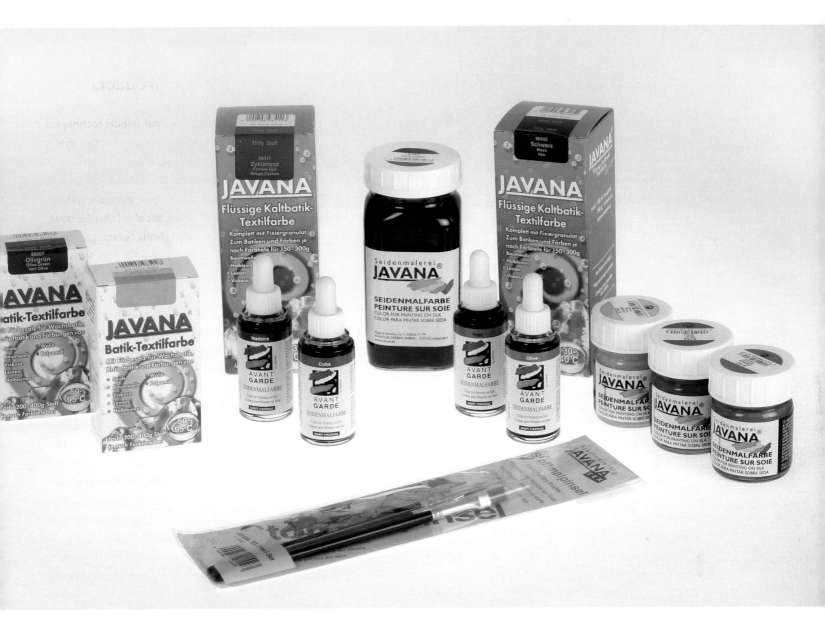

iDye colours and iDye Poly

iDye colours are colour packets which are simply put in the washing machine or in a pot of water, where they dissolve of their own accord. The dyeing is quick and clean because you don't need to fiddle about with powder. The colour packets, which are suitable for natural fibres such as cotton, silk, wool, linen and viscose, come in a range of 30 colours. iDye Poly colour packets for polyester and nylon are available in eight different shades.

Cold-water batik textile dye

Cold-water batik textile dyes allow the dyeing of cotton, linen/cotton mixes, linen and viscose in a dye bath at 30°C (86°F). The colour substance comes in liquid form and enables even dyeing of the material. Dye salts and fixative are included. One packet is sufficient to achieve the optimum colour with 150g (5½oz) of material.

Hot-water batik textile dye

Hot-water batik textile dye is used for silk, cotton, linen/cotton mix, wool and polyamide. It is very lightfast. The dye bath can be heated up to between 50 and 95°C (122 and 203°F). One packet is sufficient for 200g (7oz) of material. Dye salts are included.

Silk-painting colours

Silk-painting colours are very good for completely dyeing or selectively colouring all types of silk, etamine and needle fleece. Two different kinds of silk-painting colours are available: those fixed with a dry iron and those you fix by steam-ironing. Both kinds are available from the specialist supplier in a wide range of colours.

Dry-iron silk-painting colours spread nice and evenly and can be thinned down with water. To fix them you need to iron the reverse side of the fabric for a few minutes (using dry heat), thereby fusing them to the textile base. The coloured fabric will be wash-, cleaning- and light-resistant.

Steam-iron silk-painting colours are miscible one with another and demonstrate good fluid properties as well as high colour brilliance and great colour depth. The natural smoothness of the fabric is unaffected. The colours can be thinned down with water.

Textile base materials that have been painted or partially coloured with steam-iron colours must be fixed with steam for at least one and possibly several hours. Hobby and craft shops may offer steam-iron fixing services. Detailed instructions for the various colour products and how to use them always come with the packaging. For example, JAVANA colours can be used for cotton, linen and leather.

Steam-iron silk painting colours applied to silk or wool products can be fixed in a pressure cooker. To do this, roll up the painted fabric in newspaper and stick this down with masking tape. Then roll up this roll from one end to the other in a spiral shape, so that it resembles a snail shell. Line the base of the sieve in the pressure cooker compartment with aluminium foil and a thick layer of newspaper. Likewise, put newspaper around the sides of the sieve. Lay the rolled-up fabric in newspaper in the sieve, then cover it with a thick layer of newspaper. After that, to protect the fabric from condensation drops place a layer of aluminium foil on top of the top layer of newspaper. Then put about 2cm (¾in) of water in the pressure compartment underneath the sieve. Stand the sieve on a trivet in the pot. The sieve must not be standing in water, nor even touching it. The fabric item should be steamed for one hour.

Steam-iron silk-painting colours can also be used in modern shibori for quick, practicable dye baths when your goal is complete colouring of the fabric. To make a dye bath, put about three litres of water in a large and well-used cooking pot and bring it to the boil. Put your steam-iron colour in the boiling water. Now add the object to be dyed to the dye solution. The longer the fabric stays in the colour bath, the more intense the colour that results.

Note: Make sure you add enough dye to the water so that you don't get pastel tones. When the dyeing process is complete, take the fabric out of the bath and under running water wash out any excess colour then press with a dry iron. AVANTGARDE (made by C. Kreul) is suitable for dyeing wool products and silk.

Additional resources

Shibori pipes

For the Japanese arashi technique that will be introduced later in the book, you will need a pipe which will be wrapped with material. Ideal for this task are drainage pipes, which you can buy in various diameters from a plumber's merchant. Flexible aluminium pipes like the one in the photo are also excellent for this technique. They are extendable and temperature-resistant up to 200°C (392°F). The pipes are also easy to compress in length so that they can be made to fit into a bath of boiling dye solution. Flexible plastic and paper pipes are also available. They can also be used in shibori techniques that don't involve colouring.

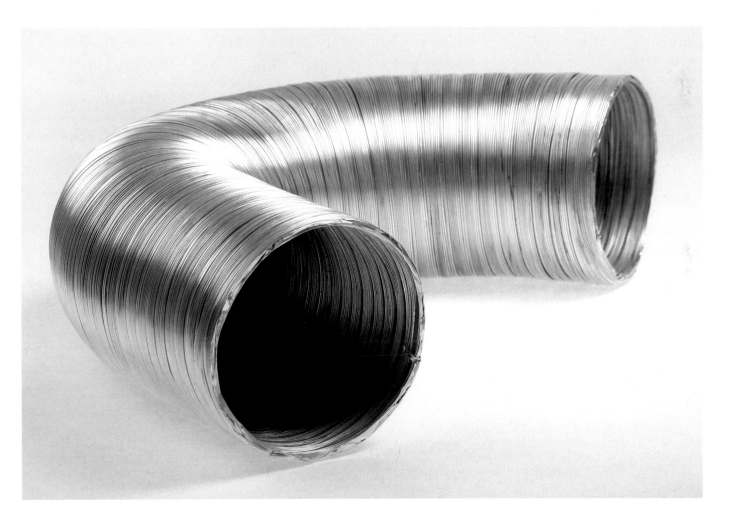

For small pieces of material that you want to make using the arashi technique, a piece of garden hose is sufficient. If you want to dye the material, then the hose needs to be heat-resistant.

Shibori sticks and bricks

For the Japanese itajime technique that is introduced later in the book, you will need two wooden sticks or bricks. In this technique, the textile or non-textile base materials are folded up concertina-style. You have to fix the folds so that you don't lose them during the dyeing process. For that you need to secure a wooden stick or brick on each side with string or with a clamp. The size of the wooden objects you use will depend on the size of the folded base material.

Scissors

Sharp, pointed scissors are essential for many shibori techniques. Long sharp fabric scissors are needed for cutting textile and non-textile base materials to the size you want. Short, handy scissors are needed to cut off the binding threads but also to pick them off carefully once the textile piece is finished.

Some strings lie very close to the base material, which makes them difficult to remove. Embroidery or nail scissors are very useful in this instance.

Washing machine

The washing machine is a wonderful device to use with numerous modern shibori techniques, so that, for example, three-dimensional structures can be fixed permanently in textile base materials. You can also dye fabric quickly and uncomplicatedly using a standard washing machine; you don't need a sophisticated model for modern shibori. Use good-quality dye products and you will get an attractive end result.

Paintbrushes

Good brushes for use on textile pieces don't need to be expensive. Basically, you can use two different kinds: decorator's brushes and flat artist's brushes. You can manage well with three basic brush thicknesses: fine, medium and large. For rapid painting of large surfaces it is best to use a foam roller or a wider brush (2–3cm/¾– 1¼in). When you're buying brushes, look for a clean point on the brush and a seamless metal holder.

All brushes should be cleaned up under running water after use. Never leave a brush standing in a jar of water, as this will probably distort its shape.

Needles and knitting needles

Sewing needles are used in modern shibori for joining two materials – in the main this means fabrics sewn together with thread. The needle size should be appropriate for both the fabric and the thread.

Safety pins are useful for provisional joining together of pieces of textile or non-textile materials. They are ideal for this task as they don't slip out. In shibori they are used as an additional resource, but they can also be left in the material permanently as aesthetic objects in their own right.

Pins are normally used for joining together two materials provisionally, before they are sewn together. Pins can be used in modern shibori as an added resource, but they can also be inserted into the piece to create an effect. Pins with coloured or different-shaped heads can be a very attractive feature in a shibori piece.

Knitting needles

Wool knitted with knitting needles can look more refined when worked on with shibori techniques, as you can see from the various knitted objects in this book. These objects were mainly knitted with needles of between 12 and 20mm (roughly speaking, between US sizes 17 and 35). It is important when using wool in shibori that the type of wool you have can be felted in the washing machine. If you so desire, you can use both wool that shrinks or has been shrunk and wool with a Superwash rating (it can be washed in the machine on a 60°C/140°F wool cycle setting) in one and the same shibori object.

SHIBORI TECHNIQUES

Plangi

One technique, many meanings. These words encapsulate the wonderful appeal of plangi, an Indonesian term meaning 'to wrap around'. The same technique is known in Japan as 'kanoko shibori' and in Nigeria as 'adire eleso'.

Basic plangi technique

The basic technique consists of binding a textile or non-textile base. The binding can be done with a simple thread or string, but also with a metallic thread, and either simply and spontaneously, without any particular plan, or following a more complex design. If you like, the textile base can also be wholly or partially dyed. Those places on the work that are bound with thread will not take on any colour.

The basic technique involves twisting the textile or non-textile base and wrapping around the bit you have twisted three or four times with thread. You can repeat this procedure as many times as you like. Once the first object has been bound, you can break the string and secure the binding with a double knot. Alternatively, continue binding with the same string or thread from one object to the next.

You can vary this basic technique as you incorporate filling or stuffing materials such as stones, pearls and pulses, or you can fold the textile or non-textile base, with one layer on top of another, then bind it.

Variation 1

Lay the textile or non-textile base over the filling material (e.g. a stone), then twist the base material to enclose the object and wrap it three or four times with thread. Then lay the next filling material under the base and follow the same procedure.

Break the string after you have bound the first filling object and secure each bound object with a double knot. Alternatively, you can carry on binding further objects with the same piece of string or thread.

Step 1

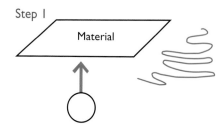

Material

Step 2

The filling material can be either left in or removed from the textile or non-textile base, depending on the purpose you intend for your shibori piece.

Variation 2

Within a given piece, stuffing materials can be worked into the front or reverse sides of textile or non-textile bases. In this way, the shibori art object is given the appearance of three-dimensional depth not only on the front side, but on both sides.

Variation 3

In this variation the fabric is simply folded up concertina-style, whereupon you bind up the sections you have chosen to gather, with or without filling.

TECHNIQUES

Variation 3

Step 1

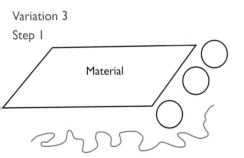

Material

Step 2

Shibori beads   Binding thread

Variation 4

With the end of a pencil, press the textile or non-textile base into a cone shape. Hold the base tightly about 2cm (¾in) up the pencil shaft from where it pushes up the base surface, then take out the pencil and wrap thread around the cone shapes in one or more different places.

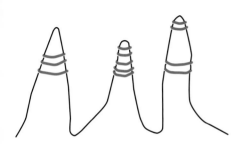

Arashi

'Storm' would be the free translation of the meaning of the Japanese term 'arashi shibori', conveying a positive sense of how the end result appears.

Basic arashi technique

Traditionally, this technique would have been realised with a felled tree trunk, in most cases with a length of 3–5m (10–16ft) and a diameter of 20cm (8in). Standing your tree trunk on end, you would have wrapped the material around it and dyed it in that position.

In modern shibori you should wrap your textile base diagonally around a shibori pipe (see page 25) and secure it with thread or string. The base material is wrapped tightly with binding thread, then forcefully drawn together and compressed. When wrapping the pipe, make sure that you pull the string so that it lies against the pipe at regular intervals.

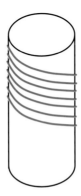

The basic technique for arashi allows you to place the pipe in a dye bath so as to dye the wrapped piece. Make sure, whether vertical or horizontal in the bath, that the whole of the pipe is immersed. Alternatively, apply the dye product to the material with a wide brush. The more intensively you apply the dye, the sooner it will penetrate the length of fabric wrapped around the pipe.

Variation 1

The textile base can be wrapped twice or even more times around the shibori pipe and then dyed.

Variation 2

Another option is to slide the textile base around the pipe and twist in one direction.

Variation 3

A further possibility would be to draw together and twist different textile bases on the same pipe in two opposing directions, as follows:

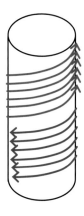

1. Wrap the material around the pipe.
2. Bind the material to the pipe with strings.
3. Now twist the tightly bound fabric around the pipe: from the upper part of the pipe twist in an anticlockwise direction towards the middle; from the middle twist in a clockwise direction to the bottom part of the pipe.

Tritik

The word 'tritik' comes from the Indonesian word meaning 'sewed'. But this technique is traditional not only in Indonesia: in Japan it is known as 'kawamaki shibori' and in Nigeria as 'adire alabere' (adire meaning 'taking, binding, colouring'; alabere meaning 'with a needle').

Tritik technique can be applied using a sewing machine, but traditionally of course it was done by hand. All the tritik works on display in this book were sewn by hand with a needle.

Basic tritik technique

The basic tritik technique is a simple running stitch, and can be employed on textile or non-textile bases. For this you need a sewing needle and appropriate tear-proof thread. The running stitch consists of evenly spaced stitches sewn in the same direction, always from right to left. This is a useful technique for fabrics where the threads in the cloth can be counted: you pass a stitch through one point and then bring it up through the back at regular intervals. For fabrics where the threads cannot be counted, you need a good eye for distances to maintain a regularly

spaced stitch. When you have finished your stitch, you need to pull the threads tight so as to gather up the textile or non-textile base.

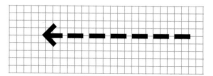

Variation 1

The prepared material can be folded over.

Variation 2

The prepared material can lie on the fold with a running stitch following the line of the fold.

Variation 3

The prepared material can be rolled up.

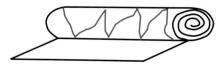

1. Roll up the fabric.
2. Apply a zigzag stitch across the width of the roll of material so that the material is sewn together along its width.

Variation 4

The running stitch can be worked out as a pattern (for example, as a floral design). As you're doing this you need to pay attention that the beginning and end threads of a pattern of, say, squares or circles can be easily pulled together or tied.

Other tritik variations

Besides tritik works that are merely sewn and dyed, there are also those using textile or non-textile bases which are first folded and then hand-sewn. These forms feature prominently in West Africa.

In some tritik techniques textile designers sometimes use a sewing machine to achieve interesting results – for example, to add a zigzag stitch.

Shibori works that combine plangi and tritik techniques look wonderful.

Itajime

Itajime shibori refers to a textile or non-textile base that is folded together concertina-style one or more times, and then bound together firmly between two wooden bricks or sticks with a tear-proof string. Then you dye the visible edges of the textile base.

The material can be folded into various forms. One way is to fold it into a triangle, of which there are two variations: right-angled and equilateral triangles. It is important when attempting these shapes to make sure the material is folded in straight lines. Ideally, you should iron the folds into the material to ensure they are clearly defined.

Another option involves folding the material concertina-style to create a rectangular three-dimensional shape. Lay a piece of wood or wooden brick on the top and bottom faces of your finished concertina object and secure the wood to the object by binding them with string.

Step 1

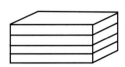

Fold up the material concertina-style to achieve a rectangular three-dimensional shape.

Step 2

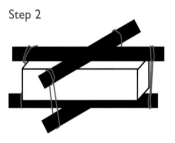

Secure the concertinaed material shape with four pieces of wood (two top and two bottom), then secure the top pieces to the bottom with string, so as to tightly compress the material shape between the wood pieces.

GALLERY OF PROJECTS

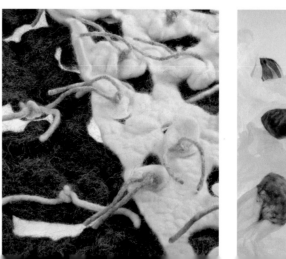

ROOTS

Material

- Undyed etamine, 90 x 150cm (35½ x 59in)
- Half a ball of dull-gold metallic thread
- Scissors
- Washing machine

Instructions

1 Cut 45–50 20cm (8in) pieces of metallic thread.

2 This project involves binding bits of material into little polyps, resembling fingers of coral, using the plangi technique without filling (plangi variation 4, page 30). On one side of the material bind 45–50 polyps clustered together following the method outlined in plangi variation 4. The rest of the surface of the material remains unworked.

3 Wash the etamine in the washing machine with a powder suitable for delicates at 30°C (86°F), so that the heat shrinks, or rather felts, the wool.

4 Dry the washed work by laying it out on a flat surface.

The edges of the etamine should not have a seam, as the action of turning it into felt through shrinking will deliver neat edges in any case. When this is done, you will have a finished material that can be readily worked on without fraying at the edges.

Depending on the colour product you choose, the finished, felted work can be dyed without the metallic thread taking on the dye colour.

GOLD

Materials

- Dong Feng silk chiffon (gauze), 90 x 90cm (35½ x 35½in)
- One ball of bright-gold metallic thread (e.g. Madeira lamé)
- Scissors

Instructions

1 Cut 40–50 12cm (4¾in) pieces of metallic thread.

2 This project entails binding bits of material into polyps, as in the previous project, using the plangi technique without filling. On one side of the material bind 40–50 polyps clustered together, following the method outlined in plangi variation 4 (see page 30). Leave one section of the surface of the silk unworked.

(see page 30)

TIP

Depending on the colour product you choose, the bound work can be dyed without the metallic thread taking on the dye colour.

AIR

Materials

- Stainless-steel silk, 200 x 400cm (78¾ x 157½in)
- Half a ball of binding thread
- Scissors
- Washing machine

Instructions

1 Cut about 30 20cm (8in) pieces of binding thread.

2 This project involves binding bits of material into nebulous peaks, like airy spires of whisked egg white, using the plangi technique without filling. On one side of the material bind around 30 densely clustered peaks according to the method outlined in plangi variation 4 (see page 30). The whole surface of the textile should be worked in this way.

3 Put the bound work in the washing machine at either 30°C (86°F) or 60°C (140°F). (The textile object will shrink more and become more felted at the higher temperature.)

4 After washing, let the silk dry before removing the binding thread from the work.

The bound work can be used as a shawl or for interior decoration (e.g. as a covering for a lampshade).

SCENT

Materials

- Mulberry-coloured etamine,
  90 x 180cm (35½ x 71in)
- One ball of binding thread
- Scissors
- Washing machine

Instructions

1 Cut 30 15cm (6in) pieces of binding thread.

2 This project entails binding bits of material into gnarled polyps using the plangi technique without filling. On one side of the material bind around 30 densely clustered polyps according to the method outlined in plangi variation 4 (see page 30). The whole surface area of the etamine should be worked in this way.

3 Wash the bound work in the washing machine at 60°C (140°F), using a powder suitable for delicates, so that the etamine shrinks into its distinctive form. Make sure when washing it at a later date that the etamine is washed with garments of a similar colour, to avoid it losing colour.

4 After washing, first let the etamine dry out slightly. Then, while it is still damp, the binding threads can be easily unwound from the wool fabric.

Plangi with wooden fillings

Dyed etamine shawl with wooden balls (dia. 2cm/¾in) bound in a wave shape.

Dyed etamine shawl with wooden balls (dia. 2cm/¾in) bound in square sections.

Dyed etamine shawl with bound wooden balls and wooden discs (dia. 2cm/¾in) arranged in diagonal rows.

Dyed etamine shawl with bound horizontal wooden dowels, c. 4cm (1½ in) long.

Plangi variation with wool felt but no filling

Plum-coloured wool felt with black/silver metallic thread binding, arranged in rows.

SKY

Materials

- Undyed etamine, 90 x 150cm (35½ x 59in)
- 100 plain wood pearls, dia. 1cm (⅜in)
- One ball of binding thread
- Scissors
- Washing machine

Instructions

1 Cut around 100 10cm (4in) pieces of binding thread.

2 This project involves binding balls into fabric using the plangi technique with filling (plangi variation 1). Bind closely together into the material around 100 wood pearls according to the method outlined in plangi variation 1 (see page 30). The whole surface area should be worked in this way.

3 Wash the bound work in the washing machine at 60°C (140°F), using a powder suitable for delicates, so that the etamine shrinks.

4 After washing, first let the etamine dry out slightly. Then, while it is still damp, the binding threads can be easily unwound from the wool fabric, and the wood pearls removed.

SKY

MOON

Materials

- Three balls of white merino wool, each about 150m (492ft) in thread length.
- One pair of 12mm (US size 17) knitting needles
- 33 wood balls, dia. c.5cm (2in)
- One ball of binding thread
- Scissors
- Washing machine

Instructions

1 First knit the shawl from the wool. This should not be completely rectangular, but can easily become wider or narrower in the same garment.

2 When the knitting is done, carefully cast off the wool thread.

3 Cut some 33 20cm (8in) pieces of binding thread.

4 Following the method outlined in plangi variation 1 (see page 30), wrap the wooden balls tightly in the knitted object and secure them with binding thread.

5 Wash the bound knitted object at 30°C (86°F) in the washing machine.

6 After that is done, remove the wooden balls from the knitted object while this is still damp and leave it to dry.

MOON

STARS

Materials

- 6 balls of silver merino wool, each about 150m (492ft) in thread length.
- One pair of 12mm (US size 17) knitting needles
- 120 wooden discs, dia. *c*.5cm (2in)
- Four balls of binding thread
- Sharp scissors
- Washing machine

Instructions

1 Knit a triangular shape out of the silver-coloured wool.

2 When this is done, cast off the wool thread.

3 Cut around 120 20cm (8in) pieces of thread.

4 Following the method outlined in plangi variation 2 (see page 30), wrap the wooden discs with wool from the front and back of the knitted triangle and bind tightly with binding thread.

5 Wash (and therefore felt) the bound knitted object in the washing machine at 30°C (86°F).

6 After washing, remove the wooden discs from the shrunk knitted object while it is still damp. To do this, make little cuts in the sides of the shrunk knitted disc forms and pull out the discs.

7 After that is done, lay out the knitted object to dry.

STARS

YIN AND
YANG

Materials

- Three balls of white wool suitable for felting
- One pair of 12mm (US size 17) knitting needles
- One ball of black wool suitable for felting
- An embroidery needle for use with the felting wool
- 20 dice-sized wooden cubes, 4 x 4cm (1½ x 1½in)
- A quarter of a ball of binding thread
- Scissors
- Washing machine

Instructions

1 Using first the white felting wool, cast 20 stitches onto your knitting needle.

2 Knit seven rows, alternating right and left stitches.

3 Cast five further stitches onto the knitting needle. Knit the row with the same stitch pattern as before. At the end of the row cast a further five stitches so that the knitted object will be a little bit wider on both sides.

4 Continue knitting as before, until all three balls of the white wool have been used up.

5 Now using the black felting wool and the embroidery needle, embroider significant areas of black stitches onto the front side of the knitted piece. To do that, embroider five diagonally placed, parallel lines in each block. Add further similar embroidered areas across the whole surface of the work.

6 Cut around 20 20cm (8in) pieces of binding thread.

7 Using binding thread, bind in the wooden dice shapes at various points in the knitted object next to the embroidered black areas, following the method outlined in plangi variation 1 (see page 30).

8 Wash the bound and embroidered knitted object at 30°C (86°F) in the washing machine.

9 Remove the binding thread from the object and lay it out to dry.

ASH

Materials

- White silk shawl (Pongee 05 silk), 30 x 150cm (11¾ x 59in)
- Half a ball of binding thread
- Black textile dye (for a dye bath)
- Sharp scissors
- Black imitation leather, 40 x 160cm (15¾ x 63in)
- Sewing needle
- Black sewing thread
- Gas or electric hob
- Old cooking pot

Instructions

1 Cut five 28cm (11in) pieces of binding thread.

2 Using the method outlined in plangi variation 4 (see page 30), with binding thread bind up five large columns, each one 12–15cm (4¾–6in) high.

3 Prepare the dye bath in the cooking pot according to the dye manufacturer's instructions, then put the bound silk in the pot for approximately 15 minutes.

4 When the silk is dyed, wash out the excess dye under running water and leave to dry.

5 As soon as the silk is completely dry, you can open up the bound plangi columns.

6 Now lay the silk on the top side of the imitation leather. At those places where there are opened-up columns, cut out circles from the imitation leather underneath. Mark out the circles before you cut if you feel that's necessary.

7 When all five openings have been cut, place the silk under the leather, so that the columns project from the openings.

8 Now using a needle and thread sew the silk to the underside of the imitation leather with tacking stitches. Make sure that the silk is well attached to the edges of the circles. The stitches should be invisible (depending on the surface quality of the imitation leather). Bear in mind that if you use a sewing machine to sew the silk to the leather, the stitches will be visible. But you can make a virtue of this effect, for example by using a metallic sewing thread in a contrasting colour.

WATER

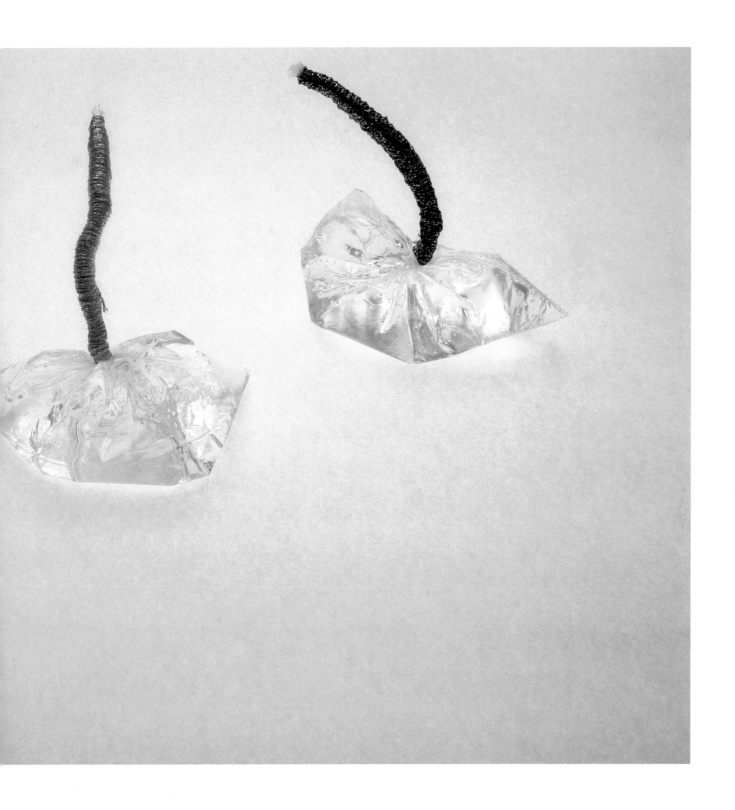

Materials

- Three transparent plastic bags
- Wool remnants in three colours
- Water

Instructions

1 Fill each plastic bag with approximately 10–15cm (4–6in) of water.

2 Twist the ends of the plastic bags together in one direction. Now bind these twisted ends tightly together with wool. You can either use the same colour wool for each bag or a different colour for each. The bound shibori objects will look attractive for about two to three weeks in a shady spot.

You can dye the water in the bags with coloured ink, and use the same colour wool to bind the bag ends.

WATER

METAL

Materials

- Dark red glass cubes, 0.5 x 0.5cm ($^3/_{16}$ x $^3/_{16}$in)
- Fine wire mesh, about 80 x 80cm (31.5 x 31.5in)
- Wire pliers

Instructions

1 Cut square pieces of wire mesh of about 5 x 5cm (2 x 2in).

2 Put a glass cube in the centre of each of these wire-mesh pieces.

3 Holding each glass cube firmly through the wire mesh, twist the wire piece so that the cube becomes lodged at the top of the manipulated shape you have created. Make sure that the bottom edges of the piece stay loose and open. In this way the wire assumes its wonderful sculptural form.

METAL

PLANT

Materials

- One packet of dried white beans
- One or two balls of black metallic thread (e.g. Madeira lamé)
- Thin transparent cover sheeting (e.g. decorator's polythene dust sheets), 200 x 300cm (79 x 118in)
- Scissors

Instructions

1 Cut 150–200 20cm (8in) pieces of metallic thread.

2 Bind the white beans in the cover sheeting with the black metallic thread following plangi variation 2. You can choose any shape you like for this piece: rectangular, square, circular or freeform.

Thread and pulses are useful resources for sculptural or pictorial objects.

LIFE

Materials

- Stainless-steel silk, *c.*200 x 400cm (79 x 158in)
- Fairytale wool in various berry tones
- Felting mat
- Felting needle
- 20 wooden balls, dia. *c.*6cm (2⅜in)
- Scissors
- One ball of binding thread
- Washing machine

Instructions

1 Using the felting mat, the felting needle and the fairytale wool, needle-felt areas of about 8 x 8cm (3⅛ x 3⅛in) across the entire surface of the silk, following the instructions laid out in the panel (right). Make sure that the felted squares are not too close to each other, i.e. they should be at least 25cm (10in) apart.

2 Cut around 20 20cm (8in) pieces of thread.

3 Lay a wooden ball on each of the felted silk areas and bind it in, following the method outlined for plangi variation 1 (see page 30).

4 Once a ball has been incorporated into each of the felted areas, wash the silk in the washing machine at 60°C (140°F), so that the felting wool felts and the silk takes on the structure of the balls.

5 After washing, dry the fabric and, having cut through the threads, carefully remove the balls from the silk.

LIFE

TIP The bound work can be worn as a shawl or used as an object for interior decoration.

DRY FELTING

Materials

- Silk
- Fairytale wool in berry tones
- Felting mat
- Felting needle

Instructions

1 Lay the wool on the silk ground and shape it with your hands into the desired form. Pierce the wool continuously with the felting needle until it has enmeshed itself with the silk base.

2 Fixing the felting needle in a wooden handle will make it easier to use. If you are planning to needle-felt large areas, it is advisable to get hold one of these handles, which can hold up to nine needles at a time, as well as a larger polystyrene sheet.

3 When this basic form has been felted, repeat the process with more felting wool until a three-dimensional form has emerged. Afterwards, you can introduce details to the felted area using thin skeins of wool applied with a felting needle.

TREE

Materials

- Silk (Pongee 05 or crêpe satin), 90 x 200cm (35½ x 78¾in)
- Shibori aluminium pipe
- One ball of binding string
- Black textile colour for silk (for a warm dye bath)
- Gas or electric hob
- Cooking pot

Instructions

1 Wrap the silk around the pipe following the instructions for the basic arashi technique (see page 31). Next dye the silk, making sure that the fabric is wrapped all the way around the pipe.

2 Make up the dye bath following the manufacturer's instructions and bring it to a simmer on the hob.

3 Put the pipe wrapped in silk in the dye bath for between 15 and 20 minutes. The pipe should not be fully immersed, so the top part of the silk will not be standing in the dye bath. However, the absorbency of the material means that the colour will rise anyway throughout the entire fabric.

4 After dyeing take the pipe out of the dye bath. Rinse the silk under running water to remove the excess dye. There are now two possibilities for the further development of the fabric.

   a) If you want to return the silk to its original, smooth state, you need to remove it from the pipe while still damp and iron it smooth.

   b) If you want a pleated structure, leave the silk on the pipe until it is completely dry and only then take it off.

TIP

As well as silk you can fashion numerous other textile bases – felt, cotton, velvet or viscose – using the arashi technique. It is important always to use a dye product specifically designed for the fabric you have chosen. Take note of the manufacturer's advice you find on the packaging.

ICE

Materials

- Painted silk crêpe satin (see panel), 90 x 150cm (35½ x 59in)
- White wool felt, 100 x 160 (39½ x 63in)
- Half a ball of black/silver metallic thread
- 60–70 white wooden balls, dia. c.2cm (¾in)
- Scissors
- Washing machine

Instructions

I Lay the wool felt under the painted silk and machine-stitch the two together using a sewing machine. You can do this either fairly freely or following a pattern.

2 Cut 60–70 pieces of metallic thread, each about 20cm (8in) long.

3 Bind the wooden balls into the silk and felt fabric following plangi variation I (see page 30).

4 Wash the bound silk/felt in the washing machine at 30°C (86°F).

5 Take the object out of the washing machine and lay it out flat for drying. The wool felt shrinks in the washing machine, which causes the work to contract so that the wooden balls stand out proudly in relief.

If you like, you can remove the wooden balls, as the metallic-thread binding is pleasing to look at on its own.

SILK PAINTING

Materials

- Silk
- Plastic film
- Dry-iron silk-painting colour, 25ml (0.85 US fl.oz)
- Iron
- Artist's paintbrush
- Water

Instructions

I Spread out the plastic film on your work surface.

2 Completely soak the silk under running water then gently press out the water.

3 Lay the damp silk on the plastic film, then at intervals pull up the fabric in small pointed spires.

4 Drop blue and black silk-painting colours at random points on the fabric. For brighter colour effects sprinkle a few drops of water onto the fabric where colour has been applied.

5 Then leave the silk to dry on your work surface.

6 Finally, fix the colour according to the manufacturer's instructions by ironing and washing the dried silk.

ICE

WOOD

Materials

- Dyed silk crêpe satin, 90 x 150cm (35½ x 59in) (see previous two projects)
- White wool felt, 100 x 160cm (39½ x 63in)
- One ball of black/silver metallic thread (e.g. Madeira lamé)
- Scissors
- Washing machine

Instructions

1 Lay the wool felt under the silk and machine-stitch the two together using a sewing machine. You can do this either fairly freely or following a pattern.

2 Cut about 30 pieces of metallic thread about 40cm (16in) long.

3 Bind the silk according to plangi variation 4 (see page 30), such that the bound columns achieve a height of about 15cm (6in).

4 Wash the bound silk in the washing machine at 30°C (86°F).

5 Take the object out of the washing machine and lay it out flat for drying. The wool felt shrinking causes the work to contract. For aesthetic reasons the metallic thread pieces should remain as part of the work.

WOOD

VALLEY

Materials

- Silk (Pongee 05), 110 x 110cm (43¼ x 43¼ in)
- 30–40 elongated, transparent plastic buttons, 1 x 10cm (⅜ x 4in)
- Half a ball of white binding thread
- Scissors
- Glass ball lamp, dia. c.25cm (10 in), with detachable metal stand

Instructions

1 Cut 30–40 pieces of thread about 12cm (4¾ in) long.

2 Space the buttons evenly on the surface of the silk and bind them into the fabric following plangi variation 1 (see page 30).

3 Drape the bound silk over the glass ball lamp and pull the ends of the materials into the metal stand.

VALLEY

TIP

White paper thread is also well-suited to binding up this ball-lamp work.

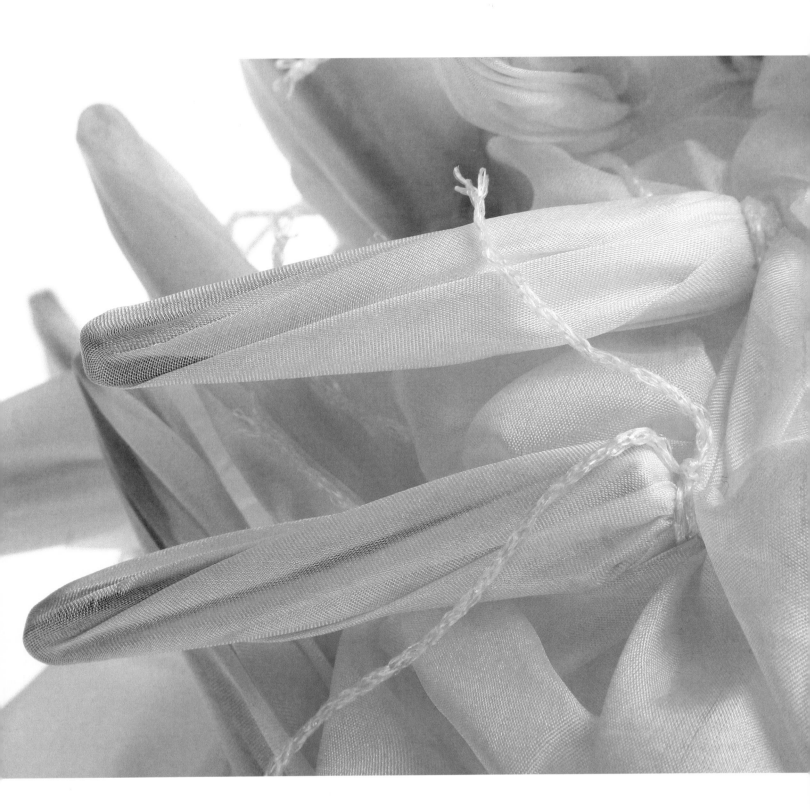

EARTH

Materials

- Silk (Pongee 05), 110 x 110cm (43¼ x 43¼ in)
- 30–40 nails, 3–4cm (1⅛–1½ in) long
- One ball of white metallic-effect thread
- Scissors
- Glass ball lamp, dia. c.25cm (10in), with detachable metal stand

Instructions

1 Cut 30–40 thread pieces about 12cm (4¾ in) long.

2 Pierce the silk with the point of a nail, from the back of the fabric through to the front.

3 Slightly twist the silk around the head of the nail, then tightly bind the nail with a piece of thread.

4 Repeat the procedure with the other nails until the whole silk base is punctured.

5 Lay the bound silk over the glass ball lamp and pull the ends of the material into the metal stand.

TIP

White paper thread can also be used for this lampshade.

EARTH

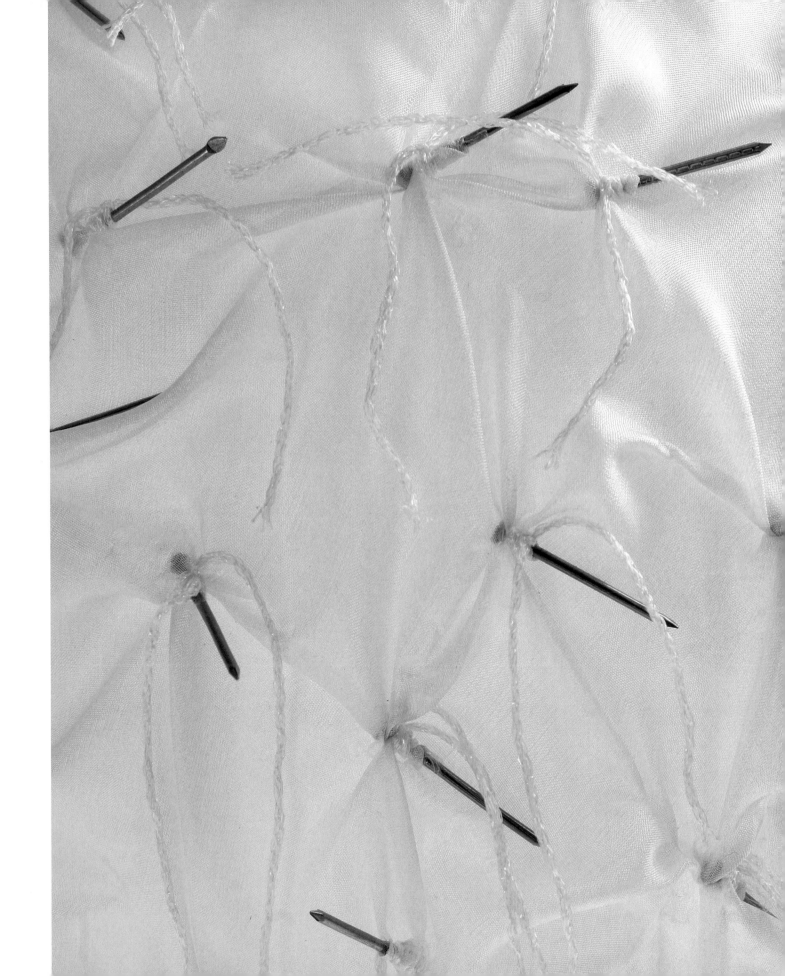

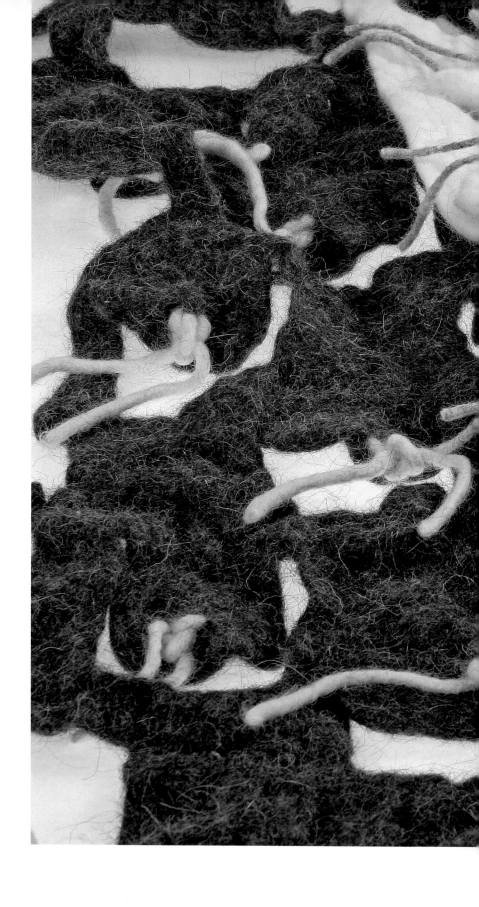

SUN

Materials

- Coarse undyed or charcoal-grey wool felt, 120 x 240cm (47¼ x 94½in)
- One roll of undyed or charcoal-grey wool wick
- Sharp needle (with a large eye)
- Scissors
- Washing machine

Instructions

1 Taking the entire piece of wool felt, cut forms in it that are reminiscent of round door openings, leaving one straight part still attached, like a hinge, to the main piece. Make sure that all the openings are cut in the same direction (i.e. the hinges should all be in the same position) but also that they vary in size.

2 Cut pieces of wool wick about 20cm (8in) long, sufficient to match the number of openings you have cut in the wool felt.

3 Thread a wool wick piece through the eye of the sharp needle.

4 Fold back one of the cut-open 'doors' in the wool felt surface (see photos on pages 114–15 and opposite). Pull the needle threaded with wool wick through the felt surface and the folded-back door, then tie a double knot at the top surface of the door.

5 Repeat steps 3 and 4 for all the doors.

6 Wash the prepared wool felt at 30°C (86°F) in washing machine.

7 After washing the object, lay it out flat to dry.

STILLNESS

Materials

- White craft felt, 45 x 400–500cm (17¾ x 155–195in)
- Steam-ironed black textile dye (for a dye bath, check how the craft felt is manufactured before choosing your dye)
- Two old cooking pots
- Plastic film

Instructions

1 Roll up the craft felt into a tight roll.

2 Prepare the dye bath in one of the cooking pots according to the manufacturer's instructions.

3 Pour some of the colour from this pot into the second pot, so that the depth of dye solution left in the first pot is only about 2–3cm (¾–1⅛in).

4 Now stand the craft-felt roll in the dye bath for five minutes. Then invert the roll and stand it on its other end in the dye bath for the same length of time. You may need to pour more of the dye solution from the second pot into the dye bath. During the dyeing process the dye is slowly absorbed by the felt and is simultaneously fixed by the rising steam.

5 Take the felt roll out of the dye bath and lay it out to dry on a well-covered surface. The felt roll should be completely dry after 3–5 days, whereupon you can roll it out to be worked on further.

A dyed felt roll looks wonderf
either as a visual object in itse
or cut into strips (see right

FIRE

Materials

- Thin white felt available by the metre, *c.*180 x 95cm (71 x 37in)
- Sharp needle
- Half a ball of white tear-proof thread
- Soft pencil
- Long ruler or strip of wood

Instructions

1 From the white thread, cut 15 threads about 250cm (98in) long.

2 Thread one through the eye of the needle.

3 On the underside of the felt draw multiple lines running parallel across the fabric. Use a ruler to ensure that the lines are straight and equally spaced.

4 Following the basic tritik technique (see page 32), sew short running stitches, about 1cm (⅜in) long, along one of the drawn lines. Make sure that the stitches on the underside run for a few centimetres before reemerging through the front.

5 With the same movement sew threads along all the previously drawn lines.

6 When all the threads are sewn, slowly and carefully pull all the thread ends, so that the felt is drawn together along these lines, concertina-style. Make sure you don't tear the threads or pull any of them out of the felt.

TIP

Classic tritik works can also be dyed, in which case use a dye-resistant thread. Put the drawn-together material in the appropriate dye bath. After drying, remove the threads from the object. In those parts of the work where previously there were threads, there will now be bright areas.

List of suppliers

Aljo Mfg. Co.
49 Walker Street, first floor
New York City
NY 10013
USA
www.aljodye.com
Synthetic dyes and other supplies

Ario
Ario 5, Pengry Road
Loughor
Swansea, SA4 6PH
UK
www.ario.co.uk
Textile and silk paints, threads, fabrics, brushes

De Witte Engel
Binnenburg 15
1791 GG
NL–Den Burg/Texel
The Netherlands
www.dewitteengel.nl
Fabric, felt

Fibrecrafts
George Well and Sons Ltd
Old Portsmouth Road
Peasmarsh, Guilford,
Surrey, GU3 1LZ
UK
www.fibrecrafts.com
Felt, silk, wool, shibori supplies

Fil Katia S.A.
Av. Catalunya s/n – Aptdo
E–138 08296 Castellbell i el Vilar
Barcelona
Spain
www.katia.es
Wool, yarn

Gütermann
Landstraße 1
D–79261 Gutach Breisgau
Germany
www.guetermann.com
Threads, yarns, textile dyes, glass and wood beads

Home Crafts Direct
PO Box 38, Leicester LE1 9BU
UK
www.homecrafts.co.uk
A range of art and craft materials

Kraftkolour P/L
PO Box 379, Whittlesea
VIC 3757
Australia
kraftkolour.com.au

Madeira
Ulrich + Michael Schmidt
& Co. GmbH
Hans-Bunte-Straße 8
D–79108 Freiburg
Germany
www.madeira.de
Fancy yarns, scissors, needles

Simply Sequins
6 Fairfield Terrace
Havant, Hants, PO9 1BA
UK
www.simplysequins.co.uk
Glass pearls, threads, ribbons, felts

Zürcher Stalder AG
Postfach
CH-3422 Kirchberg
Switzerland
www.zsag.ch
Yarn

Further reading

Belfer, Nancy, *Batik and Tie Dye Techniques* (Dover Publications Inc., New York, 1992).

Crowther-Smith, Alison, *Shibori Knitted Felt: 20 Plus Designs to Knit, Bead and Felt* (Interweave Press, Loveland, 2008).

Ellis, Catharine, *Woven Shibori (Weaver's Studio)* (Interweave Press, Loveland, 2005).

Gunner, Janice, *Shibori for Textile Artists* (Kodansha America, New York, 2007).

Southan, Mandy, *Shibori Designs & Techniques* (Search Press, Tunbridge Wells, 2008).

Wada, Y., Rice, M. & Barton, J., *Shibori: The Inventive Art of Japanese Shaped Resist Dyeing* (Kodansha International, Tokyo/New York/London, 1999).

Acknowledgements

The author would like to sincerely thank all those who have helped me to realise this book project.

Silke Bosbach is a freelance designer and author living in Oberath near Cologne. She studied art, among other things, at the University of Cologne. Since 1985 she has worked with textile art and design for couture, scarves, interior design and sacred art, as well as decoration for trade fairs and the stage. She has created designs for UNICEF and is a lecturer in textile design for an independent art school in Germany. She has written books and specialist articles, leads seminars and workshops and gives lectures in textile design.

First published in Germany by Haupt Bern

Published in Great Britain in 2011
A&C Black Publishers, an imprint of
Bloomsbury Publishing Plc
36 Soho Square
London W1D 3QY

Copyright © 2010 by Haupt Bern

ISBN: 978-1-4081-5148-8

Text and projects: Silke Bosbach
(Overath, Germany)

Photography: Birgit Völkner
(Overath, Germany) (except for photos on pages 9 and 29: Silke Bosbach)

Editorial adviser: Petra Puster, Niederpöcking, Germany

Layout and design: Susanne Nöllgen, GrafikBüro, Berlin, Germany
English translation and copy-editing: Ulla and Julian Beecroft